THE PERIPLUS OF HANNO

A VOYAGE OF DISCOVERY
DOWN THE WEST AFRICAN COAST,
BY A CARTHAGINIAN ADMIRAL
OF THE FIFTH CENTURY B.C.

TRANSLATED FROM THE GREEK

BY

WILFRED H. SCHOFF, A.M.
Secretary of the Commercial Museum, Philadelphia

With explanatory passages quoted from numerous authors

Sandycroft Publishing

The Periplus of Hanno

A Voyage of Discovery
Down the West African Coast,
By a Carthaginian Admiral
Of the Fifth Century BC.

Translated from the Greek
by
Wilfred H. Schoff, A.M.

First published 1912
This edition ©2014

Sandycroft Publishing
http://sandycroftpublishing.com

ISBN 978-1500280581

The illustration on the title page is redrawn from a Sidonian coin of the 5th century B.C, in the Hunterian Collection at Glasgow.

CONTENTS

The Voyage of Hanno, King of the Carthaginians..................1
The Geography of the Voyage of Hanno..........................5
Editions of the Periplus of Hanno.............................7
Carthaginian Chronology.......................................9
The "Burning Country" of §§ 14–16............................12
Carthage and the Carthaginians...............................13
Phœnicians and Carthaginians.................................24
The Dominion of Carthage.....................................27
The Negritos...29
Pygmies..31
Carthaginian Trading...33

LIST OF ILLUSTRATIONS

Trireme mosaic from Carthage...................................i
Map to illustrate the Periplus of Hanno........................4
The city of Carthage at its height............................11
Plan of Harbors at Carthage—after Bosworth Smith..............17
Carthage Harbor reconstruction................................23
Carthage Harbor today...23
"Dwarfs of the Southern Countries" acting as temple guards...30
From a relief in the Temple of Bubastis.......................30
Mediterranean Sailing Vessel..................................32
From a Mosaic of Carthage in the Roman Period.................32
Mediterranean Galley of the period of Hanno's Periplus........33
Redrawn from a Greek Vase in the Metropolitan Museum,
    New York..33

Trireme mosaic from Carthage

THE VOYAGE OF HANNO, KING OF THE CARTHAGINIANS

To the Libyan regions of the earth beyond the Pillars of Hercules, which he dedicated also in the Temple of Baal, affixing this

1. It pleased the Carthaginians that Hanno should voyage outside the Pillars of Hercules, and found cities of the Libyphœnicians. And he set forth with sixty ships of fifty oars, and a multitude of men and women, to the number of thirty thousand, and with wheat and other provisions.

2. After passing through the Pillars we went on and sailed for two days' journey beyond, where we founded the first city, which we called Thymiaterium; it lay in the midst of a great plain.

3. Sailing thence toward the west we came to Solois, a promontory of Libya, bristling with trees.

4 Having set up an altar here to Neptune, we proceeded again, going toward the east for half the day, until we reached a marsh lying no great way from the sea, thickly grown with tall reeds. Here also were elephants and other wild beasts feeding, in great numbers.

5. Going beyond the marsh a day's journey, we settled cities by the sea, which we called Caricus Murus, Gytta, Acra, Melitta and Arambys.

6. Sailing thence we came to the Lixus, a great river flowing from Libya. By it a wandering people, the Lixitæ, were pasturing their flocks; with whom we remained some time, becoming friends.

7. Above these folk lived unfriendly Æthiopians, dwelling in a land full of wild beasts, and shut off by great mountains, from which they say the Lixus flows, and on the mountains live men of various shapes, cave-dwellers, who, so the Lixitæ say, are fleeter of foot than horses.

8. Taking interpreters from them, we sailed twelve days toward the south along a desert, turning thence toward the east one day's sail. There, within the recess of a bay we found a small island, having a circuit of fifteen stadia; which we settled, and called it Cerne. From

The Periplus of Hanno

our journey we judged it to be situated opposite Carthage; for the voyage from Carthage to the Pillars and thence to Cerne was the same.

9. Thence, sailing by a great river whose name was Chretes, we came to a lake, which had three islands, larger than Cerne. Running a day's sail beyond these, we came to the end of the lake, above which rose great mountains, peopled by savage men wearing skins of wild beasts, who threw stones at us and prevented us from landing from our ships.

10. Sailing thence, we came to another river, very great and broad, which was full of crocodiles and hippopotami. And then we turned about and went back to Cerne.

11. Thence we sailed toward the south twelve days, following the shore, which was peopled by Æthiopians who fled from us and would not wait. And their speech the Lixitæ who were with us could not understand.

12. But on the last day we came to great wooded mountains. The wood of the trees was fragrant, and of various kinds.

13. Sailing around these mountains for two days, we came to an immense opening of the sea, from either side of which there was level ground inland; from which at night we saw fire leaping up on every side at intervals, now greater, now less.

14. Having taken in water there, we sailed along the shore for five days, until we came to a great bay, which our interpreters said was called Horn of the West. In it there was a large island, and within the island a lake of the sea, in which there was another island. Landing there during the day, we saw nothing but forests, but by night many burning fires, and we heard the sound of pipes and cymbals, and the noise of drums and a great uproar. Then fear possessed us, and the soothsayers commanded us to leave the island.

15. And then quickly sailing forth, we passed by a burning country full of fragrance, from which great torrents of fire flowed down to the sea. But the land could not be come at for the heat.

16. And we sailed along with all speed, being stricken by fear. After a journey of four days, we saw the land at night covered with flames. And in the midst there was one lofty fire, greater than the rest, which seemed to touch the stars. By day this was seen to be a very high mountain, called Chariot of the Gods.

17. Thence, sailing along by the fiery torrents for three days, we came to a bay, called Horn of the South.

18. In the recess of this bay there was an island, like the former one, having a lake, in which there was another island, full of savage men. There were women, too, in even greater number. They had hairy bodies, and the interpreters called them *Gorillæ*. When we pursued them we were unable to take any of the men; for they all escaped, by climbing the steep places and defending themselves with stones; but we took three of the women, who bit and scratched their leaders, and would not follow us. So we killed them and flayed them, and brought their skins to Carthage. For we did not voyage further, provisions failing us.

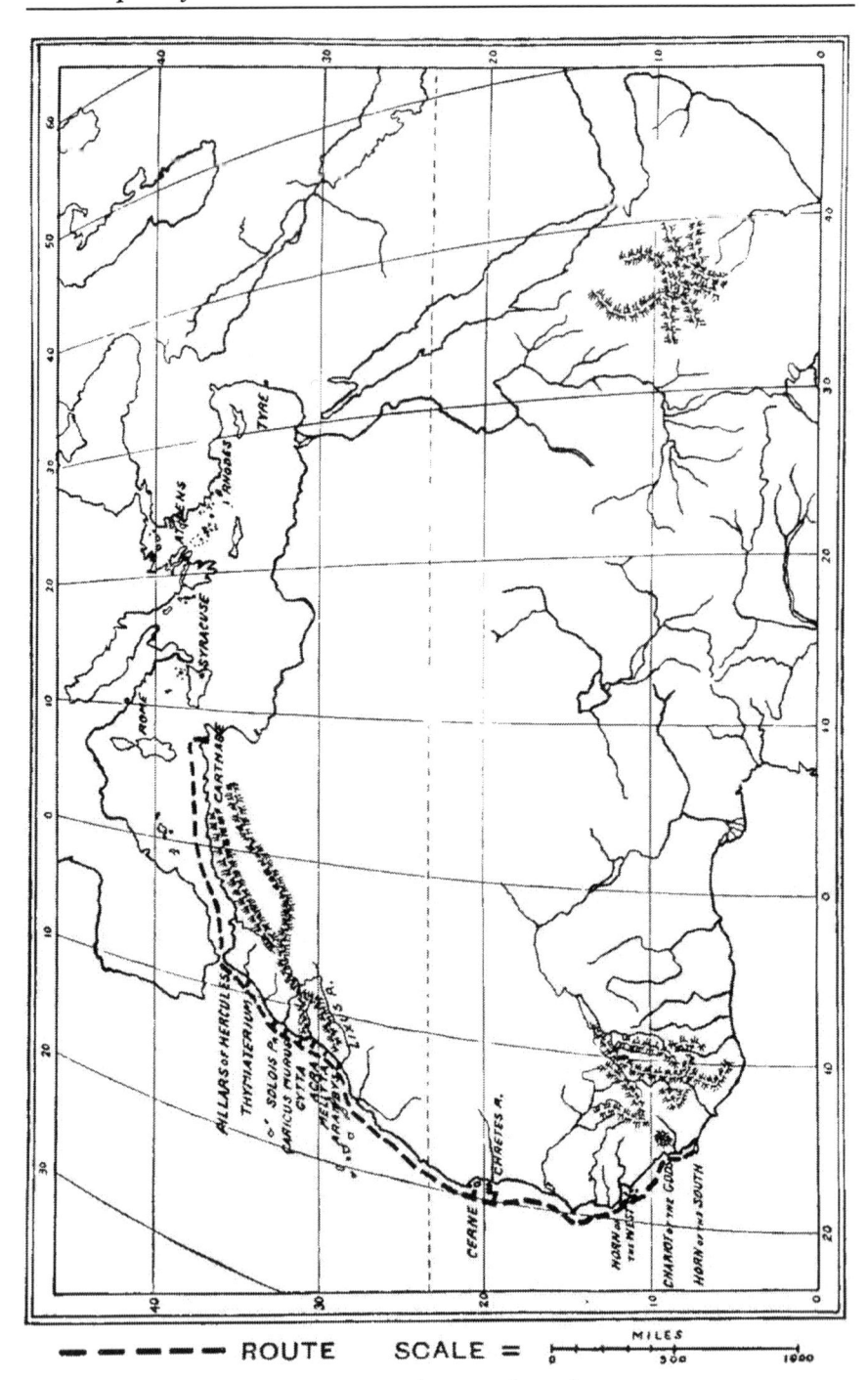

Map to illustrate The Periplus of Hanno

THE GEOGRAPHY OF THE VOYAGE OF HANNO

The Carthaginian colonies mentioned in this text can be identified only in the most general way with any existing settlement. They were destroyed and abandoned so many centuries ago that no traces are likely to remain, although the unsettled condition of the country, which has remained to the present time, has prevented any exploration of the interior or even of the coast itself.

§ 1. The Pillars of Hercules are, of course, the Straits of Gibraltar.

§ 2. The first city, called in the text Thymiaterium, is identified by Müller as Mehedia at the mouth of the Shou River at about 34° 20' N. The name of this city as we have it is a Greek corruption and to the eyes of various commentators suggests *Dumathir*—flat ground, or city of the plain.

§ 3. The Promontory of Solois is probably the same as Cape Cantin at 32° 30' N.

§ 4. The section of marshy ground is probably reached on both sides of Cape Safi, 32° 20' N.

§ 5. The location of the five colonies mentioned in this paragraph is uncertain. Müller places the first at the ruins of Agouz, 32° 5' at the mouth of the Tensift River. The second perhaps at Mogador, 31° 30'. The third at Agadir, 30° 25'. The fourth at the mouth of the Messa River, 30° 5'. The fifth, perhaps, at the mouth of the Gueder River, 29° 10', or at Araouas, 29°.

§ 6. The Lixus River is quite certainly the modern Wadi Draa, emptying into the ocean at 28° 30'.

§ 8. The island of Cerne, lying in the recess of a bay, is identified with the modern Herne Island within the mouth of the Rio de Oro at about 23° 45' N. The relative distances as mentioned in this paragraph from the Straits of Gibraltar to Carthage and to Herne Island respectively, are very nearly correct.

§ 9. The Chretes River Müller identifies with the modern St. Jean at 19° 25', at the mouth of which the three islands exist as the text describes.

The Periplus of Hanno

§ 10. The great river full of crocodiles and hippopotami is identified with the Senegal at about 16° 30' N.

§§ 12 and 13. These great wooded mountains around which the expedition sailed, can be nothing but Cape Verde, and the immense opening of the sea is the mouth of the Gambia River at 13° 30' N.

§ 14. The bay called Horn of the West reaches from 12° to 11° N. and the islands are the modern Bissagos.

§ 16. The high mountain called Chariot of the Gods, Müller identifies with Mt. Kakulima at 9° 30' N.

§§ 17 and 18. The island enclosed within the bay called Horn of the South, it is now agreed by all commentators, is the modern Sherboro Sound in the British colony of Sierra Leone, about 7° 30' N.

This identification of the places named in the text extends Hanno's voyage about 29 degrees of latitude along the West African coast, or a total length outside of Gibraltar, following the direction of the shore line, of about 2600 miles.

EDITIONS OF THE PERIPLUS OF HANNO

(From Bunbury, *History of Ancient Geography*, I, 332–3)

"The narrative of Hanno was certainly extant in Greek at an early period. It is cited in the work ascribed to Aristotle on Marvellous Narratives (§ 37) which belongs to the 3d century B.C.; as well as by Mela, Pliny, and many later writers; and Pliny expressly speaks of it as the source whence many Greek and Roman writers had derived their information, including, as he considered, many fables. (Pliny, H. N., V. 8.)

"The authenticity of the work may be considered as unquestionable. The internal evidence is conclusive upon that point. There is considerable doubt as to the date of the voyage. On this point the narrative itself gives no information, and the name Hanno was very common at Carthage. (See Smith's *Dict. of Biog.*, Art. HANNO.) But it has been generally agreed that this Hanno was either the father or the son of the Hamilcar who led the great Carthaginian expedition to Sicily in B.C. 480. In the former case the Periplus may be probably assigned to a date about B.C. 520; in the latter it must be brought down to about B.C. 470. This last view is that adopted by C. Müller in his edition of the Periplus (*Geographi Græci Minores,* I, xxi–xxiv), where the whole subject is fully discussed; but as between him and his grandfather, the choice is hardly more than conjectural.

M. Vivien de St. Martin, however, prefers the date of B.C. 570, which had been previously adopted by Bougainville (*Mémoires de l'Académie des Inscriptions,* xxviii, 287).

"The Periplus of Hanno was first published at Basle in 1533 (as an appendix to the Periplus of the Erythræan Sea), from a manuscript in the Heidelberg library (Cod. Pal. Græc, 398), the only one in which it is found. There have been numerous subsequent editions; of these the one by Falconer, 8vo, 1797, and Kluge, 8vo, Leipzig, 1829, are the most valuable. The treatise is also included in the editions of the *Geographi Græci Minores* by Hudson, Gail, and C.

Müller. The valuable and elaborate commentary by the latest editor may be considered as in a great measure superseding all others. Besides all these editions, it has been made the subject of elaborate investigations by Gosselin, Bougainville, Major Rennell, Heeren, Ukert, Vivien de St. Martin, and other geographical writers.[1] Indeed there are few ancient writings that have been the subject of more copious commentary in proportion to its very limited extent. The earliest of these commentaries, inserted by Ramusio in his collection of Voyages (Venice, 1550), is curious and interesting as being derived from Portuguese sources, who were in modern times the earliest explorers of these coasts. That by the Spanish writer Campomanes (in his *Antigüedad Marítima de Cártago,* 4to, Madrid, 1756) is, on the contrary, utterly worthless."

---

[1] To this list should be added the Histories of Ancient Geography by Bunbury (1883) and Tozer (1897).

CARTHAGINIAN CHRONOLOGY

	B.C.
Migration of the Phœnicians from the Persian Gulf to South Arabia and the Mediterranean, about	2800
Phœnician cities on the Mediterranean subject alternately to Babylon and Egypt. Rise of Assyria, about	1300
Greek activity and extension of Israel; fall of Troy, about	1183
Temporary weakness of both Assyria and Egypt makes possible the independence and alliance of Israel and Phœnicia,	1049–976
Phœnician colonies westward, about	1000
Founding of Carthage, about	878
At this period the Semitic commercial system centering in Mesopotamia, Phœnicia and Carthage controlled the trade of the world; continued expansion of Greece, and foundation of Greek colonies in Asia Minor and the Black Sea and westward in Italy, Sicily and Gaul,	800–600
Founding of Rome,	753
Decline of Assyria under this competition,	650
Greek colony established at Cyrene in North Africa,	631
Greek commercial agency established on the Nile,	630
Fall of Nineveh,	606
Extension of Carthaginian dominions in Africa, Sicily and Sardinia,	550
Defeat of the Carthaginians by the Greeks,	539
Fall of Babylon and rise of the Persian Empire,	538
War between Carthage and Syracuse for the possession of Sicily,	533
Change of Carthaginian policy toward African tribes and enforcement of tribute,	533
Rome under Etruscan kings extends its dominion in Italy,	528
Egypt conquered by the Persians,	525
Cyrene, and Africa as far as the Carthaginian possessions, conquered by the Persians,	524

Invasion of Italy by the Gauls,	520
Northern India conquered by the Persians,	512
Expulsion of the Tarquins and establishment of the Republic of Rome,	509
The Persians advance into Thrace,	505
Persian advance continues into Greece until checked by the defeat of Marathon,	490
Second effort of the older civilization against Greece under Xerxes, this time employing all its forces from India in the east to Carthage in the west, ends in double victory by the Greeks over the Carthaginians at Himera in Sicily and over the Persians at Salamis,	480
Battle of Plataea; expulsion of the Persians from Greece,	479
Probable date of the voyage of Hanno, marking the decline of Carthaginian supremacy in the northern Mediterranean and the movement to extend its trade westward by the Atlantic Ocean,	470

At this period Carthage was by far the richest city on the Mediterranean.

Invasion of Italy by the Gauls, capture and destruction of Rome,	390
Defeat of the Etruscans by the Romans,	310
Defeat of the Samnites, Nubians and Gauls by the Romans,	295
Invasion of Italy by Pyrrhus and his defeat by the Romans,	280–275
Basis of Roman wealth and power laid by the capture and sack of Tarentum,	272
First Punic war ending in the loss of Sicily to Rome,	264–241
Second Punic war ending in the loss of Spain, Sardinia and Corsica to Rome,	218–201
Third Punic war ending in the total destruction of Carthaginian power,	149–146
Capture and destruction of both Carthage and Corinth and transfer of their wealth to Rome,	146
Steady advance of Roman power in all directions ending with complete possession of the Mediterranean at the death of Augustus,	A.D. 13

The city of Carthage at its height.

THE "BURNING COUNTRY" OF §§ 14–16

Mungo Park (*Travels in the Interior Districts of Africa*. London, 1799: Chap, xx), thus describes the burning of the grass in the dry season in Senegambia:

"The termination of the rainy season is likewise attended with violent tornadoes; after which the wind shifts to the northeast, and continues to blow from that quarter during the rest of the year. . . . The grass soon becomes dry and withered, the rivers subside very rapidly, and many of the trees shed their leaves. . . . This wind, in passing over the great desert of Sahara, acquires a very strong attraction for humidity, and parches up everything exposed to the current. Whenever the grass is sufficiently dry, the Negroes set it on fire; but in Ludamar and other Moorish countries this practice is not allowed, for it is on the withered stubble that the Moors feed their cattle until the return of the rains. The burning of the grass in Manding exhibits a scene of terrific grandeur. In the middle of the night, I could see the plains and mountains, as far as my eye could reach, variegated with lines of fire; and the light reflected on the sky made the heavens appear in a blaze. In the daytime pillars of smoke were seen in every direction; while the birds of prey were observed hovering round the conflagration and pouncing down upon the snakes, lizards, and other reptiles, which attempted to escape from the flames. This annual burning is soon followed by a fresh and sweet verdure, and the country is thereby rendered more healthful and pleasant."

See also a paper by Dr. Walther Busse in *Mitteilungen aus der Deutschen Schutzgehieten*, 1908, No. 2, reviewed in the *Geographical Journal* for October, 1908.

CARTHAGE AND THE CARTHAGINIANS

By R. BOSWORTH SMITH, M. A. London, 1877
Chapter I. Extracts

"The land-locked sea, the eastern extremity of which washes the shores of Phœnicia proper, connecting as it does three continents, and abounding in deep gulfs, in fine harbors, and in fertile islands, seems to have been intended by nature for the early development of commerce and colonization. By robbing the ocean of half its mystery and more than half its terrors, it allured the timid mariner, even as the eagle does her young, from headland on to headland, or from islet to islet, till it became the highway of the nations of the ancient world; and the products of each of the countries whose shores it laves became the common property of all. At a very early period the Etruscans, for instance, that mysterious people who then occupied with their settlements Campania and Cisalpine Gaul, as well as that extensive intermediate region to which they afterwards gave their name, swept all the Italian seas with their galleys, half piratical, and half commercial. The Greeks, somewhat later, founded (B.C. 631) Cyrene and (B.C. 560) Barca in Africa, (B.C. 564) Alalia in Corsica, and (B.C. 600) Massilia in Gaul, and lined the southern shores of Italy and the western shores of Asia Minor with that fringe of colonies which were so soon to eclipse in prosperity and power their parent cities. Even Egypt, with her immemorial antiquity and her exclusive civilization, deigned to open (B.C. 550) an emporium at Naucratis for the ships and commerce of the Greeks, creatures of yesterday as they must have seemed in comparison with her.

"But in this general race of enterprise and commerce among the nations which bordered on the Mediterranean, it is to the Phœnicians that unquestionably belongs the foremost place. In the dimmest dawn of history, many centuries before the Greeks had set foot in Asia Minor or in Italy, before even they had settled down in secure possession of their own territories, we hear of Phœnician settlements in Asia Minor and in Greece itself, in Africa, in Macedon, and in Spain. There is hardly an island in the Mediterranean which has not preserved some traces of these early visitors; Cyprus, Rhodes and Crete in the Levant; Malta, Sicily, and the Balearic Isles in the middle passage; Sardinia, Corsica, and Elba in the Tyrrhenian Sea; the Cyclades, as Thucydides tells us, in the mid-Ægean; and even Samothrace and Thasos at its northern extremity, where Herodotus, to use his own forcible expression, himself saw a whole mountain 'turned upside down' by their mining energy; all have either yielded Phœnician coins and inscriptions, have retained Phœnician proper names and legends, or possess mines, long, perhaps, disused, but which were worked as none but Phœnicians ever worked them. And among the Phœnician factories which dotted the whole southern shore of the Mediterranean, from the east end of the Greater Syrtis even to the Pillars of Hercules, there was one which, from a concurrence of circumstances, was destined rapidly to outstrip all the others, to make herself their acknowledged head, to become the Queen of the Mediterranean, and, in some sense, of the Ocean beyond, and for a space of over a hundred years, to maintain a deadly and not an unequal contest with the future mistress of the world.

"The rising African factory was known to its inhabitants by the name of Kirjath-Hadeschath, or New Town, to distinguish it from the much older settlement of Utica, of which it may have been, to some extent, an offshoot. The Greeks, when they came to know of its existence, called it Karchedon, and the Romans Carthago. The date of its foundation is uncertain; but the current tradition refers it to a period about a hundred years before the founding of Rome.

"In her origin, at least, Carthage seems to have been, like other Phœnician settlements, a mere commercial factory. Her inhabitants cultivated friendly relations with the natives, looked upon themselves as tenants at will rather than owners of the soil, and, as such, cheerfully paid a rent to the African Berbers for the ground covered by their dwellings. Thus much, if thus much only, of truth is contained in the legend of Dido, which, adorned as it has been by the genius of Virgil, and resting in part on early local traditions, must always remain indissolubly bound up with the name of Carthage.

"It was the instinct of self-preservation alone which, in the course of the sixth century, dictated a change of policy at Carthage, and transformed her peace-loving mercantile community into the war-like and conquering state, of which the whole of the western Mediterranean was so soon to feel the power. A people far less keen-sighted than the Phœnicians must have discerned that it was their very existence which was at stake; at all events, unless they were willing to be dislodged from Africa, and Sicily, and Spain, as they had already been dislodged from Italy and Greece and the islands of the Levant, by the flood of Hellenic colonization, they must alter their policy. Accordingly they joined hands (in B.C. 537) with their inveterate enemies, the Etruscans, to prevent a threatened settlement of some exiled Phocæans on the important island of Corsica. In Africa they took up arms to make the inhabitants of Cyrene feel that it was towards Egypt or the interior, not towards Carthage, that they must look for an extension of their boundaries; and in Sicily, by withdrawing half voluntarily from the eastern side of the island in which the Greeks had settled, they tightened their grip upon the western portion which, as being nearer to Carthage, was more important to them, and where the original Phœnician settlements of Panormus, Motye, and Soloeis had been planted.

"The result of this change of policy was that the western half of the Mediterranean became, with one exception, what the whole of it had once bidden fair to be—a Phœnician lake, in which no foreign merchantmen dared to show themselves. It was a vast preserve, to be caught trespassing upon which, so Strabo tells us, on the authority of Eratosthenes, ensured the punishment of instant death by drowning. No promontory was so barren, no islet so insignificant, as to escape the jealous and ever watchful eye of the Carthaginians. In Corsica, if they could not get any firm or extensive foothold themselves, they at least prevented any other state from doing the like. Into their hands fell, in spite of the ambitious dreams of Persian kings and the aspirations of patriot Greeks, that greatest of all islands, the island of Sardinia; theirs were the Ægatian and the Liparæan, the Balearic and the Pityusian Isles; theirs the tiny Elba, with its inexhaustible supply of metals; theirs, too, Malta still remained, an outpost pushed far into the domain of other advancing enemies, a memorial of what once had been, and, perhaps, to the sanguine Carthaginian temperament, an earnest of what might be again hereafter. Above all the Phœnician settlements in Spain, at the innermost corner of the great preserve, with the adjacent silver mines which gave to these settlements their peculiar value, were now trebly safe from all intruders.

"Elated, as it would seem, by their naval successes, which were hardly of their own seeking, the Carthaginians thought that they might now at least become the owners of the small strip of African territory which they had hitherto seemed to occupy on sufferance only, and they refused the ground-rent which, up till now, they had paid to the adjoining tribes. Step by step they enlarged their territories at the expense of the natives, till the whole of the rich territory watered by the Bagradas became theirs. The Nomadic tribes were beaten back beyond the river Triton into the country named, from the roving habits of its inhabitants, Numidia, or into the desert of Tripolis, and were henceforward kept in check by the primitive defence of a line of ditch and rampart, just as, in earlier times, the rich plains of Babylonia had been protected by the 'wall of Semiramis' from the incursions of the less civilized Medes. The agricultural tribes were forced to pay tribute to the conquerors for the right of cultivating their own soil or to shed their blood on the field of battle in the prosecution of further conquests from the tribes beyond.

"Nor did the kindred Phœnician settlements in the adjoining parts of Africa escape unscathed. Utica alone, owing probably to her antiquity and to the semi-parental relation in which she stood to Carthage, was allowed to retain her walls and full equality of rights with the rising power; but Hippo Zarytus, and Adrumetum, the greater and the lesser Leptis, were compelled to pull down their walls and acknowledge the supremacy of the Carthaginian city. All along the northern coast of Africa the original Phœnician settlers, and, probably, to some extent, the Carthaginians themselves, had intermarried with the natives. The product of these marriages was that numerous class of Libyphœnicians which proved to be so important in the history of the Carthaginian colonization and conquest; a class which, equidistant from the Berbers on the one hand, and from the Carthaginians proper on the other, and composed of those who were neither wholly citizens nor yet wholly aliens, experienced the lot of most half castes, and were alternately trusted and feared, pampered and oppressed, loved and hated, by the ruling state.

"The original monarchical constitution—doubtless inherited from Tyre—was represented (practically in Aristotle's time, and theoretically to the latest period) by two supreme magistrates called by the Romans *Suffetes*. Their name is the same as the Hebrew

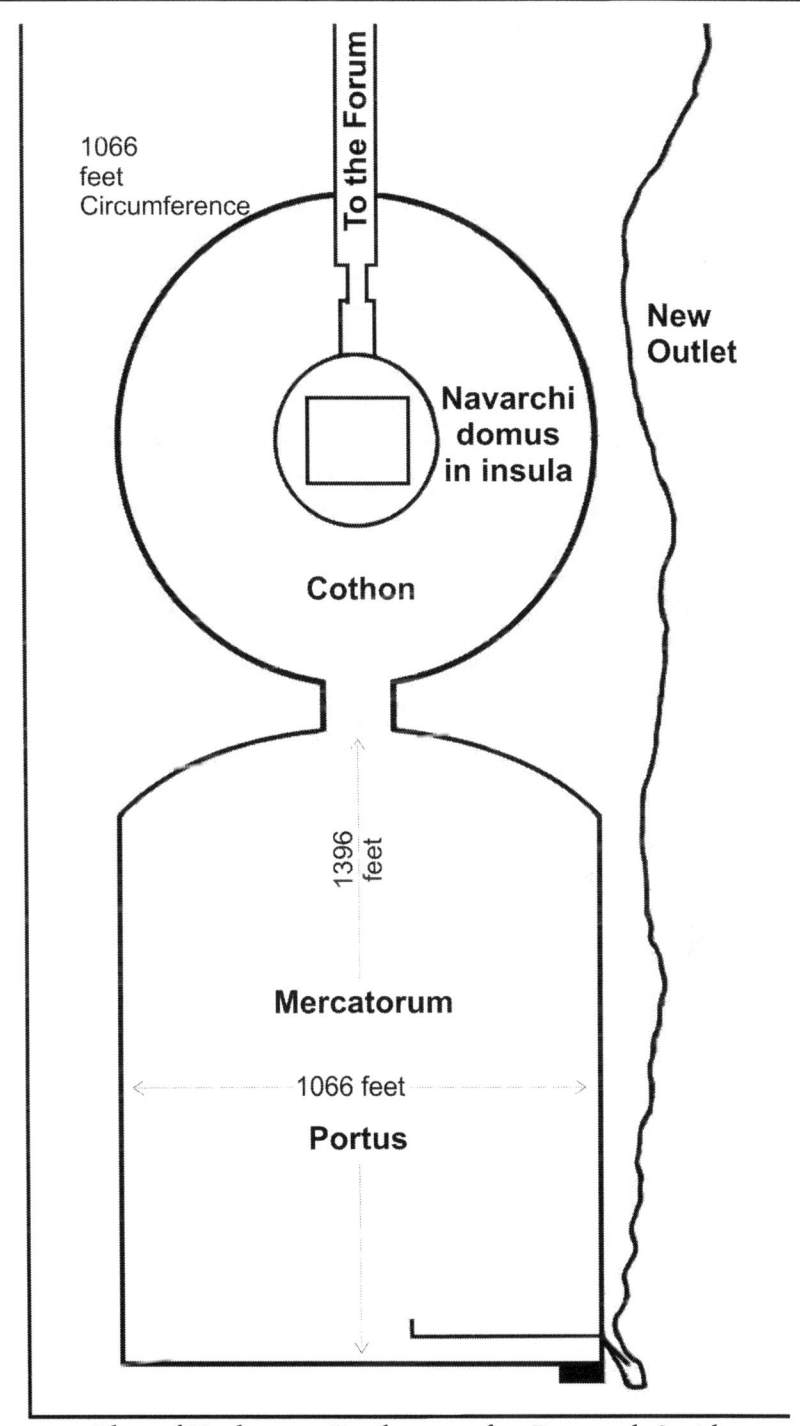

Plan of Harbors at Carthage—after Bosworth Smith

Shofetim, mistranslated in our Bible, Judges. The Hamilcars and Hannos of Carthage were, like their prototypes, the Gideons and the Samsons of the Book of Judges, and not so much the judges, as the protectors of their respective states. They are compared by Greek writers to the two kings of Sparta, and by the Romans to their own consuls. That they were in the earliest times appointed for life, and not, as is commonly supposed, elected annually, is clear from a variety of indications; and, like the 'king of the sacrifices' at Rome, and the 'king archon' at Athens, they seem, when the kingly office itself was abolished, to have retained those priestly functions which, according to ancient conceptions, were indissolubly united with royalty.

"Carthage was, beyond doubt, the richest city of antiquity. Her ships were to be found on all known seas, and there was probably no important product, animal, vegetable, or mineral, of the ancient world, which did not find its way into her harbours and pass through the hands of her citizens. But her commercial policy was not more far-sighted or more liberal than has been that of other commercial states, even till very modern times. Free trade was unknown to her; it would have seemed indeed like a contradiction in terms. If she admitted foreign merchantmen by treaty to her own harbour, she took care by the same document jealously to exclude them from the more important harbours of her dependencies. She allowed her colonies to trade only so far as suited her own immediate interests, and the precautions she took made it impossible for any one of them ever to become a great center of commerce, still less to dream of taking her place.

"But the most important factor in the history of a people—especially if it be a Semitic people—is its religion. The religion of the Carthaginians was what their race, their language, and their history would lead us to expect. It was, with slight modification, the religion of the Canaanites, the religion, that is, which, in spite of the purer Monotheism of the Hebrews and the higher teaching of their prophets, so long exercised a fatal fascination over the great bulk of the Hebrew race. The Phœnician religion has been defined to be 'a deification of the powers of Nature, which naturally developed into an adoration of the objects in which those powers seemed most active.' Of this adoration the Sun and Moon were the primary objects. The Sun can either create or destroy; he can give life or take it away. The Moon is his consort; she can neither create nor destroy, but she can receive and develop, and, as the queen of night, she presides alike over its stillness and its orgies. Each of these ruling deities, Baal-Moloch or the Sun-god, and the horned Astarte or the crescent Moon worshipped at Carthage, it would seem, under the name of Tanith, would thus have an ennobling as well as a degrading, a more cheerful as well as a more gloomy aspect. Unfortunately, it was the gloomy and debasing side of their worship which tended to predominate alike in Phœnicia proper and in the greatest of the Phœnician colonies.

"But there was one of these inferior gods who stood in such a peculiar relation to Carthage, and whose worship seems to have been so much more genial and so much more spiritual than the rest, that we are fain to dwell upon it as a foil to what has preceded. This god was Melcarth, that is *Melech-Kirjath,* or the king of the city; he is called by the Greeks 'the Phœnician Hercules,' and his name itself has passed, with a slight alteration, into Greek mythology as Melicertes. The city of which he was pre-eminently the god was Tyre. There he had a magnificent temple, which was visited for antiquarian purposes by Herodotus. . . . At Carthage Melcarth had not even a temple. The whole city was his temple, and he refused to be localized in any particular part of it. He received, there is reason to believe, no sacrifices of blood; and it was his comparatively pure and spiritual worship which, as we see repeatedly in Carthaginian history, formed a chief link in the chain that bound the parent to the various daughter-cities scattered over the coasts and islands of the Mediterranean. The Carthaginian proper names which have come down to us form one among many proofs of the depth of their religious feelings, for they are all, or nearly all, compounded with the name of one or other of their chief gods. Hamilcar is he whom Melcarth protects; Hasdrubal is he whose help is in Baal; Hannibal, the Hanniel of the Bible, the grace of Baal; and so on with Bomilcar, Himilco, Ethbaal, Maherbal, Adherbal, and Mastanabal.

"But if the life of the great capitalists of Carthage was as brilliant as we have described it, how did it fare with the poorer citizens, with those whom we call the masses, till we sometimes forget that they are made up of individual units? If we know little of the rich, how much less do we know of the poor of Carthage and her dependencies? The city population, with the exception—a large exception doubtless—of those engaged in commerce, well contented, as it would seem, like the

Romans under the Empire, if nothing deprived them of their bread and their amusement, went on eating and marrying and multiplying until their numbers became excessive, and then they were shipped off by the prudence of their rulers to found colonies in other parts of Africa or in Spain. Their natural leaders, or, as probably more often happened, the bankrupt members of the aristocracy, would take the command of the colony, and obtain free leave, in return for their services, to enrich themselves by the plunder of the adjoining tribes.

"To so vast an extent did Carthage carry out the modern principle of relieving herself of a superfluous population and at the same time of extending her empire, by colonization, that, on one occasion, the admiral Hanno, whose 'Periplus' still remains, was dispatched with sixty ships of war of fifty oars each, and with a total of not less than thirty thousand half-caste emigrants on board, for the purpose of founding colonies on the shores of the ocean beyond the Pillars of Hercules.

"But the document recording this voyage is of an interest so unique, being the one relic of Carthaginian literature which has come down to us entire, that we must dwell for a moment on its contents. It was posted up by the admiral himself, as a thank-offering, in the temple of Baal, on his return from his adventurous voyage, the first attempt, made by the Phœnicians to reach the equator from the northwest of Africa. It is preserved to us in a Greek translation only, the work probably of some inquisitive Greek traveller, some nameless Herodotus who went wandering over the world like his matchless fellow-countryman, his notebook always in his hand, and always jotting down everything that was of interest to himself, or might be of importance to posterity.

"What was the general nature of the Carthaginian trade in the distant regions thrown open to them we happen to know from another ancient writer whose authority is beyond dispute. There was in Libya—so the Carthaginians told Herodotus—beyond the Pillars of Hercules, an inhabited region where they used to unload their cargoes, and leave them on the beach. After they had returned to their ships and kindled a fire there, the natives, seeing the rising column of smoke, ventured down to the beach, and depositing by the merchandise what they considered to be its equivalent in gold, withdrew in their turn to their homes. Once more the Carthaginians disembarked, and if they were satisfied with the gold they found, they carried it off with them, and the dumb bargain was complete. If not, they returned a second time to their ships to give the natives the chance of offering more. The law of honor was strictly observed by both parties; for neither would the Carthaginians touch the gold till it amounted, in their opinion, to the full value of the merchandise; nor would the natives touch the merchandise till the Carthaginians had clinched the transaction by carrying off the gold.

"This strange story, long looked upon as fabulous, has, like many other strange stories in Herodotus, been proved by the concurrent testimony of modern travelers to be an accurate account of the dumb trade which still exists in many parts of Africa, and which traversing even the Great Desert, brings the Marroquin into close commercial relations with the Negro, and supplies the great Mohammedan kingdoms of the Soudan with the products of the Mediterranean. It proves also that the gold-fields of the Niger, so imperfectly known to us even now, were well known to the Carthaginians, and that the gold-dust with which the natives of Ashanti lately purchased the retreat of the European invader was the recognized medium of exchange in the days of the father of history.

"To defray the expenses of this vast system of exploration and colonization, as well as of their enormous armies, the most ruinous tribute was imposed and enacted with unsparing rigor from the subject native states, and no slight one either from the cognate Phœnician cities. The taxes paid by the natives sometimes amounted to a half of their whole produce, and among the Phœnician dependent cities themselves we know that the lesser Leptis alone paid into the Carthaginian treasury the sum of a talent daily. The tribute levied on the conquered Africans was paid in kind, as is the case with the rayahs of Turkey to the present day, and its apportionment and collection were doubtless liable to the same abuses and gave rise to the same enormities as those of which Europe has lately heard so much. Hence arose that universal disaffection, or rather that deadly hatred, on the part of her foreign subjects, and even of the Phœnician dependencies, towards Carthage on which every invader of Africa could safely count as his surest support. Hence the case with which Agathocles, with his small army of fifteen thousand men, could overrun the open country, and the monotonous uniformity with which he entered, one after another, two hundred towns, which Carthaginian jealousy had deprived of their walls, hardly needing to strike a blow. Hence, too, the horrors of the revolt of the outraged Libyan mercenaries, supported as it was by the free-will contributions of their golden ornaments by the Libyan women, who hated their oppressors as perhaps women only can, and which is known in history by the name of the 'War without Truce,' or the 'Inexpiable War.'

"It must, however, he borne in mind that the inherent differences of manners, language, and race between the natives of Africa and the Phœnician incomer were so great; the African was so unimpressible, and the Phœnician was so little disposed to understand, or to assimilate himself to his surroundings, that even if the Carthaginian government had been conducted with any equity, and the taxes levied with a moderation which we know was far from being the case, a gulf profound and impassable must probably have always separated the two peoples. This was the fundamental, the ineradicable weakness of the Carthaginian Empire, and in the long run outbalanced all the advantages obtained for her by her natives, her ports and her well-stocked treasury; by the energy and the valour of her citizens; and by the consummate genius of three, at least, of her generals. It is this, and this alone, which in some measure reconciles us to the melancholy, nay, the hateful termination of the struggle, on the history of which we are about to enter;

> Men are we, and must grieve when e'en the name
> Of that which once was great has passed away.

But if under the conditions of ancient society, and the savagery of the warfare which is tolerated, there was an unavoidable necessity for either Rome or Carthage to perish utterly, we must admit, in spite of the sympathy which the brilliancy of the Carthaginian civilization, the heroism of Hamilcar and Hannibal, and the tragic catastrophe itself call forth, that it was well for the human race that the blow fell on Carthage rather than on Rome. A universal Carthaginian empire could have done for the world, as far as we can see, nothing comparable to that which the Roman universal empire did for it. It would not have melted down national antipathies, it would not have given a common literature or language, it would not have prepared the way for a higher civilization and an infinitely purer religion. Still less would it have built up that majestic fabric of law which forms the basis of the legislation of all the states of Modern Europe and America."

Carthage and the Carthaginians

Carthage Harbor reconstruction

Carthage Harbor today

PHŒNICIANS AND CARTHAGINIANS

"The Phœnicians for some centuries confined their navigation within the limits of the Mediterranean, the Propontis, and the Euxine, land-locked seas, which are tideless and far less rough than the open ocean. But before the time of Solomon they had passed the Pillars of Hercules and affronted the dangers of the Atlantic. Their frail and small vessels, scarcely bigger than modern fishing-smacks, proceeded southwards along the West African coast, as far as the tract watered by the Gambia and Senegal, while northwards they coasted along Spain, braved the heavy seas of the Bay of Biscay, and passing Cape Finisterre, ventured across the mouth of the English Channel to the Cassiterides. Singularly, from the West African shore, they boldly steered for the Fortunate Islands (the Canaries), visible from certain elevated points of the coast, though at 170 miles distance. Whether they proceeded further, in the south to the Azores, Madeira, and the Cape Verde Islands, in the north to the coast of Holland, and across the German Ocean to the Baltic, we regard as uncertain. It is possible that from time to time some of the more adventurous of their traders may have reached thus far; but their regular, settled and established navigation did not, we believe, extend beyond the Scilly Islands and coast of Cornwall to the northwest, and to the southwest Cape Non and the Canaries. The commerce of the Phœnicians was carried on to a large extent by land, though principally by sea. It appears from the famous chapter (xxvii) of Ezekiel which describes the richness and greatness of Tyre in the 6th century B.C., that almost the whole of Western Asia was penetrated by the Phœnician caravans, and laid under contribution to increase the wealth of the Phœnician trader. ... Translating this glorious burst of poetry into prose, we find the following countries mentioned as carrying on an active trade with the Phœnician metropolis: Northern Syria, Syria of Damascus, Judah and the land of Israel, Egypt, Arabia, Babylonia, Assyria, Upper Mesopotamia, Armenia, Central Asia Minor, Ionia, Cyprus, Hellas or Greece, and Spain."—G. Rawlinson, *History of Phœnicia*, ch. 9.

"Though the invincible industry and enterprise of the Phœnicians maintained them as a people of importance down to the period of the Roman empire, yet the period of their widest range and greatest efficiency is to be sought much earlier—anterior to 700 B.C. In these remote times they and their colonists (the Carthaginians especially) were the exclusive navigators of the Mediterranean; the rise of the Greek maritime settlements banished their commerce to a great degree from the Ægean Sea, and embarrassed it even in the more westerly waters. Their colonial establishments were formed in Africa, Sicily, Sardinia, the Balearic Isles and Spain. The greatness as well as the antiquity of Carthage, Utica, and Gades, attest the long-sighted plans of Phœnician traders, even in days anterior to the first Olympiad. We trace the wealth and industry of Tyre, and the distant navigation of her vessels through the Red Sea and along the coast of Arabia, back to the days of David and Solomon. And as neither Egyptians, Assyrians, Persians or Indians addressed themselves to a sea-faring life, so it seems that both the importation and the distribution of the products of India and Arabia into Western Asia and Europe were performed by the Idumæan Arabs between Petra and the Red Sea—by the Arabs of Gerrha on the Persian Gulf, joined as they were in later times by a body of Chaldæan exiles from Babylonia –and by the more enterprising Phœnicians of Tyre and Sidon in these two seas as well as in the Mediterranean."—G. Grote, *History of Greece*, pt. 2, ch. 18.

"The commerce of Carthage may be conveniently considered under its two great branches—the trade with Africa and the trade with Europe. The trade with Africa . . . was carried on with the barbarous tribes of the inland country that could be reached by caravans, and of the sea-coast. Of both we hear something from Herodotus, the writer who furnishes us with most of our knowledge about these parts of the ancient world. . . . The goods with which the Carthaginian merchants traded with the African tribes were doubtless such as those which civilized nations have always used in their dealings with savages. Cheap finery, gaudily colored clothes, and arms of inferior quality, would probably be their staple. Salt, too, would be an important article. . . . The articles which they would receive in exchange for their goods are easily enumerated. In the first place comes . . . gold. Carthage seems to have had always at hand an abundant supply of the precious metal for use, whether as money or as plate. Next to gold would come slaves. . . . Ivory must have been another article of Carthaginian trade, though we hear little about it. The Greeks used it extensively in art. . . . Precious stones seem to have been another article which the savages gave in exchange for the goods they coveted. . . . Perhaps we may add dates to the list of articles obtained from the interior. The European trade dealt, of course, partly with the things already mentioned, and partly with other articles for which the Carthaginian merchants acted as carriers, so to speak, from one part of the Mediterranean to another. Lipara, and the other volcanic islands near the extremity of Italy, produced resin; Agrigentum, and possibly other cities of Sicily, traded in sulphur brought down from the region of Etna; wine was produced in many of the Mediterranean countries. Wax and honey were the staple goods of Corsica. Corsican slaves, too, were highly valued. The iron of Elba, the fruit and the cattle of the Balearic islands, and to go further, the tin and copper of Britain, and even amber from the Baltic, were articles of Carthaginian commerce. Trade was carried on not only with the dwellers on the coast, but with inland tribes. Thus goods were transported across Spain to the interior of Gaul, the jealousy of Massilia (Marseilles) not permitting the Carthaginians to have any trading stations on the northern coast of that country."— A. J. Church and A. Filman, *The Story of Carthage,* pt. 3, ch. 3.

THE DOMINION OF CARTHAGE

"All our positive information, scanty as it is, about Carthage and her institutions, relates to the fourth, third and second centuries B.C.; yet it may be held to justify presumptive conclusions as to the fifth century B.C., especially in reference to the general system pursued. The maximum of her power was attained before her first war with Rome, which began in 364 B.C.; the first and second Punic wars both of them greatly reduced her strength and dominion. Yet in spite of such reduction we learn that about 150 B.C. shortly before the third Punic war, which ended in the capture and depopulation of the city, not less than 700,000 were computed in it, as occupants of a fortified circumference of above twenty miles, covering a peninsula with its isthmus. Upon this isthmus its citadel Byrsa was situated, surrounded by a triple wall of its own, and crowned at its summit by a magnificent temple of Esculapius. The numerous population is the more remarkable, since Utica (a considerable city, colonized from Phœnicia more anciently than even Carthage itself, and always independent of the Carthaginians, though in the condition of an inferior and discontented ally) was within the distance of seven miles of Carthage on the one side, and Tunis seemingly not much further off on the other. Even at that time, too, the Carthaginians are said to have possessed 300 tributary cities in Libya. Yet this was but a small fraction of the prodigious empire which had belonged to them certainly in the fourth century B.C., and in all probability also between 480–410 B.C. That empire extended eastward as far as the Altars of the Philæni, near the Greater Syrtis,—westward all along the coast to the Pillars of Herakles and the western coast of Morocco. The line of coast southeast of Carthage, as far as the bay called the Lesser Syrtis, was proverbial (under the name of Byzacium and the Emporia) for its fertility. Along this extensive line were distributed indigenous Libyan tribes, living by agriculture; and a mixed population called Liby-Phœnician. . . . Of the Liby-Phœnician towns the number is not known to us, but it must have been prodigiously great. . . . A few of the towns along the coast—Hippo, Utica, Adrumetum, Thapsus, Leptis, etc.—were colonies from Tyre, like Carthage itself. Yet the

Carthaginians contrived in time to render every town tributary, with the exception of Utica. . . . At one time, immediately after the first Punic war, they took from the rural cultivators as much as one-half of their produce, and doubled at one stroke the tribute levied upon the towns. . . . The native Carthaginians, though encouraged by honorary marks to undertake military service were generally averse to it, and sparingly employed. . . . A chosen division of 2,500 citizens, men of wealth and family, formed what was called the Sacred Band of Carthage, distinguished for their bravery in the field as well as for the splendour of their arms, and the gold and silver plate which formed part of their baggage. We shall find these citizen troops occasionally employed on service in Sicily; but most part of the Carthaginian army consists of Gauls, Iberians, Libyans, etc., a mingled host got together for the occasion, discordant in language as well as in customs."—G. Grote, *History of Greece,* pt. 2, ch. 81.

THE NEGRITOS
(THE HAIRY PEOPLE OF § 18)

"We have seen that the African pygmies probably reached Europe during the Stone Ages, and were certainly frequent visitors at the Courts of the Pharaohs. At present they are all denizens of the woodlands, everywhere keeping to the shelter of the Welle, Ituri, Ruwenzori, Congo, and Ogoway forests within the tropics. To this may be due the fact that they are not black but of a yellowish colour with reddish-brown woolly head, somewhat hairy body, and extremely low stature ranging from 3 ft. (Lugard) to perhaps 4 ft. 6 in. at most. The hirsuteness and dwarfish size were already noticed two thousand five hundred years ago by the Carthaginian Admiral Hanno to whom we owe the term *gorilla* applied by him, not to the anthropoid ape so named by Du Chaillu, but to certain hairy little people seen by him on the west coast—probably the ancestors of the dwarfs still surviving in the Ogoway district.

"Here they are called Abongo and Obongo, and elsewhere are known by different names—Tikitiki, Akka, or Wochua in the Welle region, Dume in Gallaland, Wandorobo in Masailand, Batwa south of the Congo, and many others. Dr. Ludwig Wolf connects the Batwa both with the northern Akka and the southern Bushmen, all being the scattered fragments of a primeval dwarfish race to be regarded as the true aborigines of equatorial Africa. They live exclusively by the chase and the preparation of palm-wine, hence are regarded by their Bantu friends as benevolent little people whose special mission is to provide the surrounding tribes with game and palm-wine in exchange for manioc, maize, and bananas.

"Many are distinguished by sharp powers of observation, amazing talent for mimicry, and a good memory. Junker describes the comic ways and nimble action of an Akka who imitated with marvelous fidelity the peculiarities of persons he had once seen—Moslems at prayer, Emin Pasha with his 'four eyes' (spectacles), another in a towering rage, storming and abusing everybody, and Junker himself, 'whom he took off to the life, rehearsing down to the minutest details, and with surprising accuracy, my anthropometric performance when measuring his body at Rumbek four years before.'"—A. H. Keane, *The World's Peoples*, pp. 148–9.

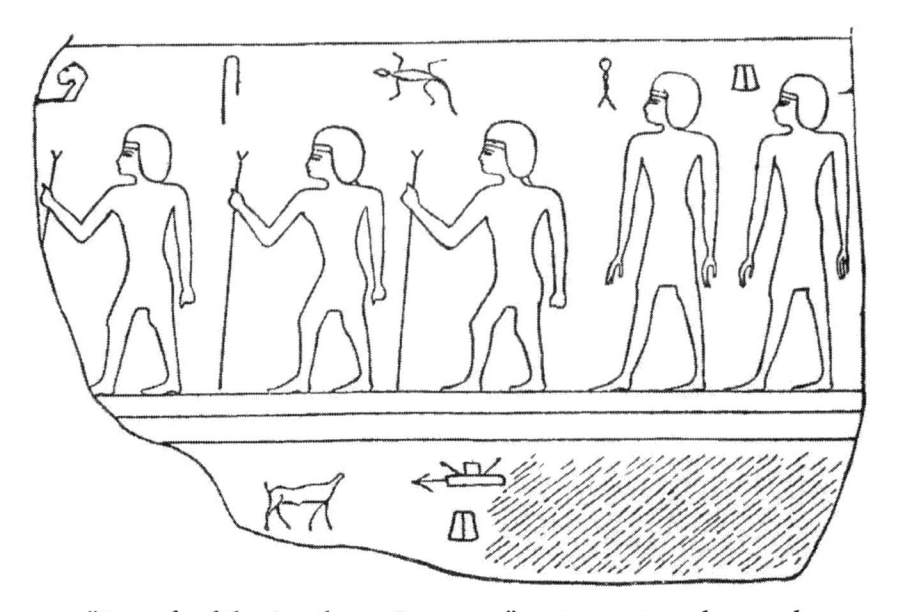

"Dwarfs of the Southern Countries" acting as temple guards. From a relief in the Temple of Bubastis.

PYGMIES

Homer, *Iliad III*, 6 —Chapman's translation:

"At all parts like the cranes that fill, with harsh confusion.
Of brutish clanges all the air and in ridiculous war
(Eschewing the unsuffer'd storms, shot from the winter's star),
Visit the ocean, and confer the Pygmei soldiers' death."

Aristotle: "The cranes go up as far as the lakes above Egypt, where the Nile originates; there the pygmies are living; and this is not a fable, but pure truth; men and horses are, as they say, of small stature, and live in grottoes."

Karnak temple, Ptolemaic era—of the nome of Nubia: "The dwarfs of the southern countries come to him, bringing their tributes to his treasury."

H. M. Stanley, *In Darkest Africa*, Vol. ii, *passim:* On pages 40–42, describing a couple of pygmies, one of whom, a man about 21 years old, measuring 4 feet in height, he observes:

"This was the first full-grown man we had seen. His color was coppery, the fell over the body was almost feathery, being nearly half an inch in length. His headdress was a bonnet of priestly form, decorated with a bunch of parrot feathers; . . .

"Twenty-six centuries ago his ancestors captured the five young Nassamonian explorers, and made merry with them at their villages on the banks of the Niger. Even as long as forty centuries ago they were known as pygmies, and the famous battle between them and the storks was rendered into song. On every map since Hecatæus' time, 500 years B.C., they have been located in the region of the Mountains of the Moon. When Mesu led the children of Jacob out of Goshen, they reigned over Darkest Africa undisputed lords: they are there yet, while countless dynasties of Egypt and Assyria, Persia, Greece and Rome, have flourished for comparatively brief periods, and expired. And these little people have roamed far and wide during the elapsed centuries. From the Niger banks, with successive waves of larger migrants, they have come hither to pitch their leafy huts

The Periplus of Hanno

in the unknown recesses of the forest. Their kinsmen are known as Bushmen in Cape Colony, as Watwa in the basin of the Lulungu, as Akka in Monbuttu, as Balia by the Mabodé, as Wambutti in the Ihuru basin, and as Batwa under the shadows of the Lunæ Montes."

*Mediterranean Sailing Vessel
From a Mosaic of Carthage in the Roman Period
In the Museum of the University of Pennsylvania, Philadelphia*

CARTHAGINIAN TRADING

Herodotus, iv, 196:

"The Carthaginians further say that beyond the Pillars of Hercules there is a region of Libya, and men who inhabit it; when they arrive among these people and have unloaded their merchandise, they set it in order on the shore, go on board their ships and make a great smoke; that the inhabitants, seeing the smoke, come down to the sea, and then deposit gold in exchange for the merchandise, and withdraw to some distance from the merchandise; that the Carthaginians, going ashore, examine the gold, and if the quantity seems sufficient for the merchandise, take it up and sail away; but if it is not sufficient, they go on board their ships again and wait; the natives then approach and deposit more gold, until they have satisfied them; neither party ever wrongs the other; for they do not touch the gold before it is made adequate to the value of the merchandise, nor do the natives touch the merchandise before the other party has taken the gold."

Mediterranean Galley of the period of Hanno's Periplus
Redrawn from a Greek Vase in the Metropolitan Museum, New York

Made in the USA
San Bernardino, CA
07 April 2019